Sergei Ankushev

Easy French Horn Lessons for Beginners

Quick Teaching Method from Simple to Complex.
Theory and Practice.
With Online Audio & Accompaniment

ISBN: 978-1-962612-25-8

Messages about typos, errors, inaccuracies and suggestions for
improving the quality are gratefully received at:
albinaopen@gmail.com

CONTENTS

A Note from the Author 5

Origin 6

Section 1. Structure and Care. Posture. Fingering 8

Section 2. Basics of Music Notation.. 14

Section 3. Breathing. Breathing Exercises................................. 19

Section 4. Structure and Types of Mouthpieces........................ 21

Section 5. *Détaché*. Whole, Half and Quarter Notes. The 3/4 Time Signature 25

Section 6. Tonality. C major.. 30

Section 7. B♭ major. *Legato*. D major....................................... 38

Section 8. *Staccato*. Eighth Notes. F major 47

Songs

As under the Hill, under the Mountain 33

Don't Fly, the Nightingale 34

A Fox.. 34

A Little Polka 35

Alegretto 35

Pop! Goes the Weasel 37

Song (M. Milman) 41

Jingle Bells... 44

Shepherd Boy... 50

Old MacDonald Had a Farm... 51

The Chicken Dance... 52

Scarborough Fair.. 54

Red River Valley 55

The Flower of Miracles 56

Songs with Accompaniment

Down in the Valley...57

Let Him Go 58

Let My People Go 59

Take Me Out to the Ball Game 60

All Audio and Video...62

A Note from the Author

Greetings!

When I began writing this book, I found myself pondering an important question: "How can I share the wonders of this fascinating instrument and not overwhelm you with unnecessary jargon?" I've aimed to strike a balance between simplified self-guided lessons and more professional techniques. I hope I was successful.

I structured this manual in such a way that it progresses from simple to complex concepts, making it accessible to anyone, even if you're new to reading music. By the end of this tutorial, you will have mastered all the **basic** skills needed to play the French horn. If you would like to further improve your performance level, I recommend that you contact a teacher.

It's important to note that training on this instrument usually starts at around age 9 or 10. This is because playing the French horn requires a certain level of physical fitness, and younger players may struggle to hold the instrument. That is why there are many smaller types of French horns.

It is essential to follow the sequence of the sections. I strongly advise against skipping any parts if you are a complete beginner with no prior knowledge or skills.

Sergei Ankushev

Origin

French horn (<u>German</u> *Waldhorn* — 'forest horn', <u>Italian</u> *corno*, <u>French</u> *cor*) is a brass wind instrument used in symphony orchestras.

It originated from a hunting horn and was first used in an orchestra by Jean-Baptiste Lully in 1664. Until the 1830s, like other brass instruments, it had no valves and was a natural instrument with a limited range. This was the so-called natural horn, which was used in classical and baroque music, including by Bach, Mozart, and Beethoven.

A single (three-valve) French horn is available in a single key—either in F great octave, which was historically the main key of the French horn known for its beautiful sound, or in the higher B/B-flat (♭) great octave.

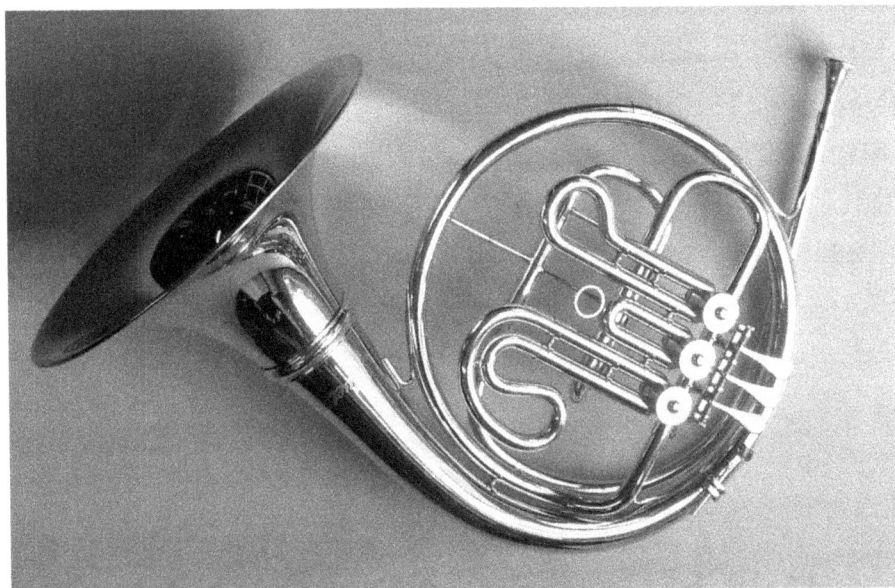

A double (four-valve) French horn has two **pitches**, F and B. Using the fourth valve, the F **pitch** can be switched to B, or, depending on the design of the horn, vice versa—the B **pitch** can be switched to F. The B **pitch** was added to the F horn to facilitate the performance of upper register notes.

Many contemporary jazz French horn players rose to fame in the 70s, 80s, 90s, and 2000s. These include Robert Rausch, Adam Ainsworth, Jim Rattigan, Richard Todd, Arkady Shilkloper, Giovanni Hoffer, Sharon Freeman, Peter Gordon, and Marshall Sealy.

Section 1.
Structure and Care. Posture. Fingering

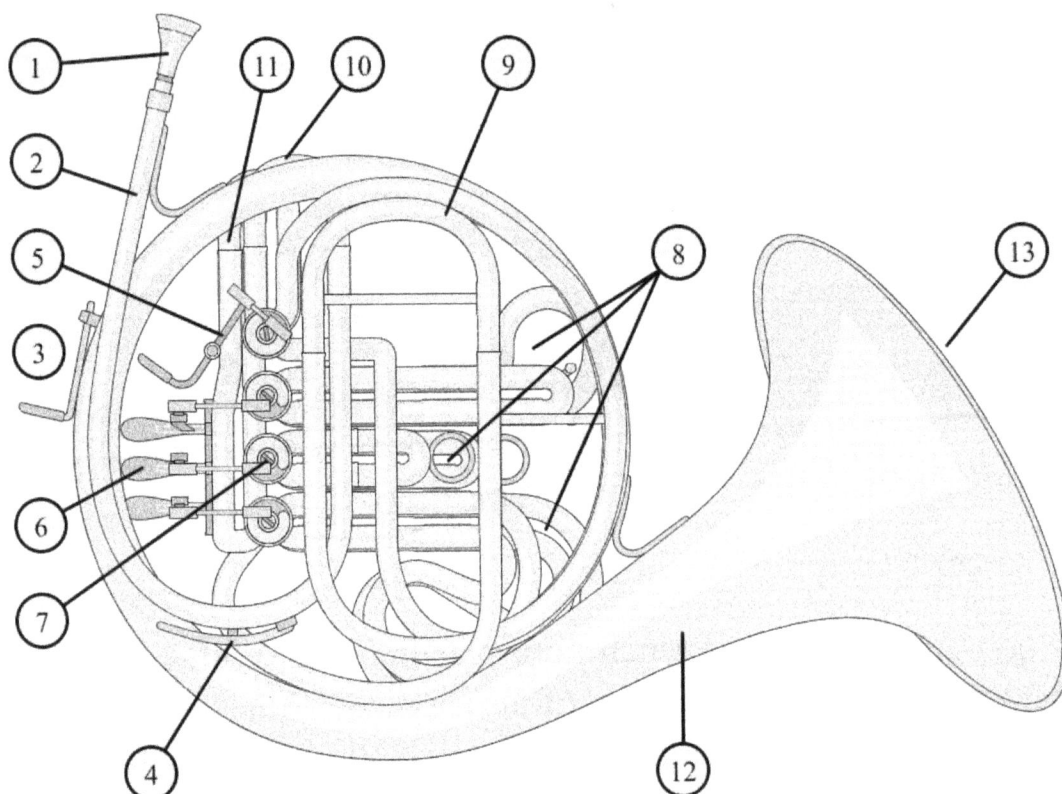

1. **The mouthpiece** is necessary for extracting sound. They come in different sizes and structures. Mouthpieces are covered in section 4.

2. **The leadpipe**—the mouthpiece goes into it.

3. Adjustable handrest.

4. **Water key** is used to allow the drainage of accumulated fluid. Our breath contains moisture that condenses inside the instrument during performance. This liquid interferes with sound production and should be occasionally drained. That is the purpose of **the water key.**

5. The fourth valve is used for switching between F and B pitches.

6. A valve lever.

7. A **rotary** valve. All **rotary** valves should be oiled approximately once a week.

8. Tuning slides used to tune the valves. They also need to be lubricated with a special thick oil.

9. Long tubing for F pitch with slide.

10. General slide is used to tune the instrument..

11. Short tubing for B♭ pitch with slide.

12. Bellpipe.

13. The bell emits the sound. It could be fixed or removable.

Posture

Complete beginners often have the illusion that it is fine to simply pick up the French horn and play. However, that is not the case. There are a few rules regarding **posture** that can save you from making serious mistakes. It's important!

Posture includes the position of the mouthpiece on the lips, the position of the body, arms, head, hand and fingers. Posture affects sound quality, expressiveness, technique (speed of performance) and endurance.

- The left arm should be as free as possible to allow for easy finger movements. The right hand is relaxed.

- The entire weight of the instrument should rest on the right arm. Below are two ways to hold a French horn by the bell.

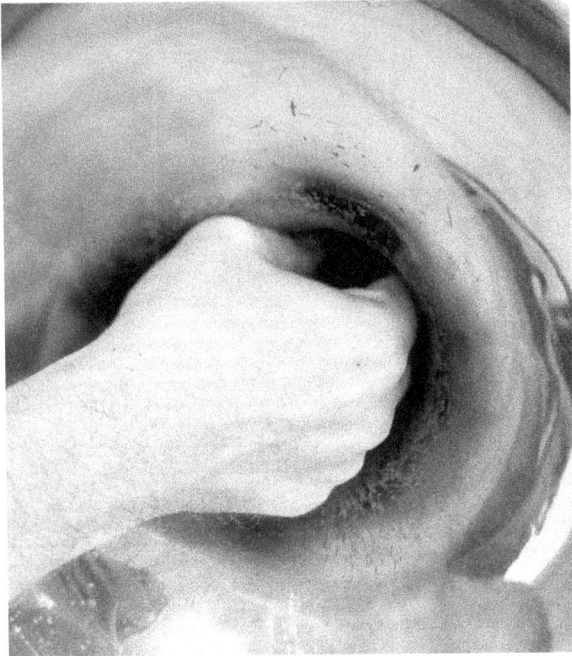
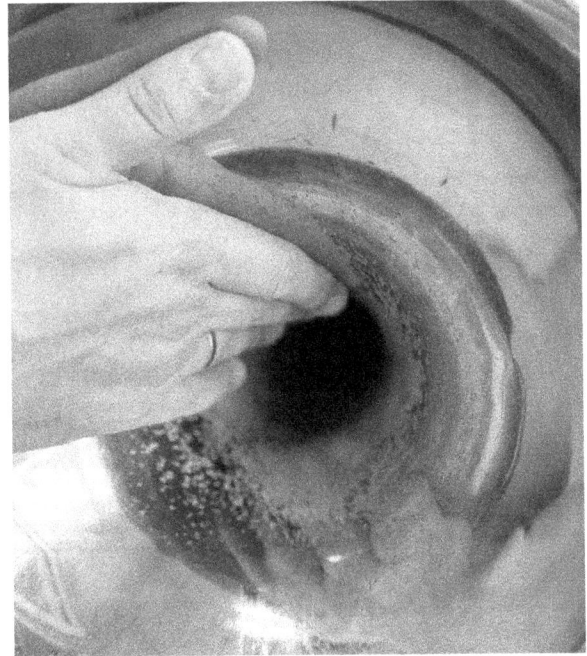

- Maintain a natural body posture. Don't hunch over or stick out your chest.
- Hold your neck straight.
- Keep your hands at a distance from the body. This is necessary so as not to restrict breathing and not to interfere with the work of the right arm.
- You can play standing and sitting.

- **Make sure that your fingers are in their proper places.**

Fingering

F	2	0		23	12	1	2	0	12	1	2	0	1
B	123	13		23	12	1	2	0	23	12	1	2	0	

Gb G♮ G# Ab A♮ A# Bb B♮ C C# Db D♮ D# Eb E♮ F♮

F	2	0	23	12	1	2	0	12(2)	1(0)	2	0	1
B	12	1	23	12	1	2	0	23	12	1	2	0	

F# Gb G♮ G# Ab A♮ A# Bb B♮ C♮ C# Db D♮ D# Eb E♮ F♮

The French horn can produce either a B pitch or an F pitch, which is why there are two fingering variants. Often, the horn is equipped with a fourth valve, used to switch between these pitches. This provides the player with a choice of fingerings, allowing for greater convenience and flexibility in playing.

No fingers (indicated by 0). No need to press anything.

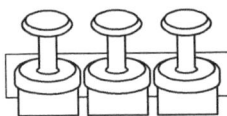

The 2nd finger.

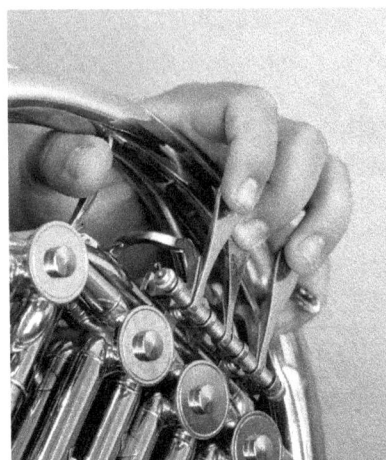

The 1st finger.

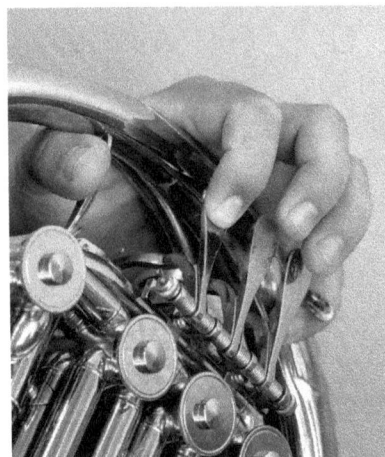

The 1st and 2nd fingers, indicated by 12.

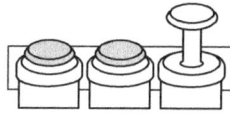

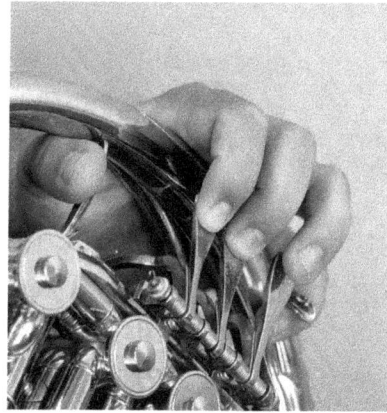

The 2nd and 3rd fingers, indicated by 23.

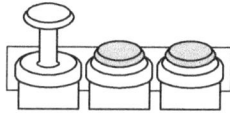

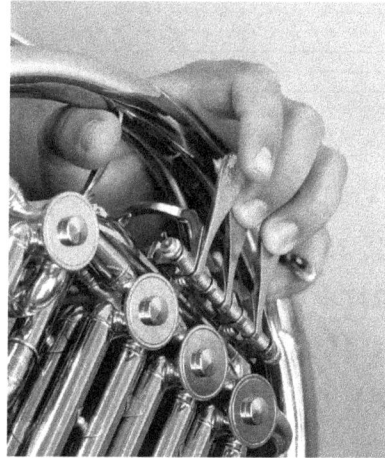

The 1st and 3rd fingers, indicated by 13.

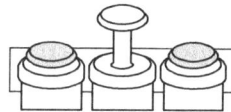

The 1st, 2nd and 3rd fingers, indicated by 123.

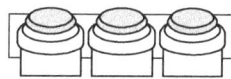

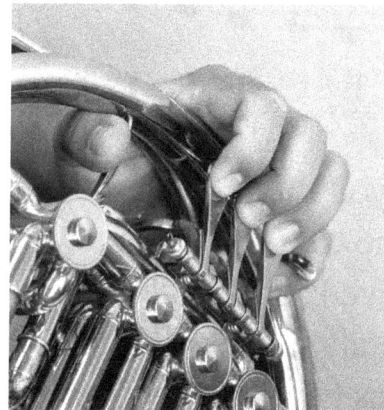

Section 2.
Basics of Music Notation

It's time for you to get acquainted with the ocean of musical notation. We are not going to dive in deep, just to dip our toes in.

Notes are written on a 5-line **stave (or staff)**.

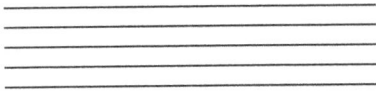

You've probably wondered why there are only 7 notes and so many sounds. The fact is that there are 7 note names, but there are different **OCTAVES: sub contra (C0), contra (C1), great (C2), small (C3), the 1st line (C4), the 2nd line (C5), the 3rd line (C6), the 4th line (C7) and a little bit of the 5th line (C8).** Lower sounds are commonly referred to as **INFRASOUND**. Higher sounds are called **ULTRASOUND**.

Human hearing is limited to less than the full nine octaves. Many animals (dogs, bats, dolphins, etc.) recognize sounds much higher. The focus of this tutorial is three octaves: the great (C2), small (C3) and 1st line (C4) octaves. You will start with the small octave and gradually expand your performance range. The image shows the approximate range of a beginning French horn player.

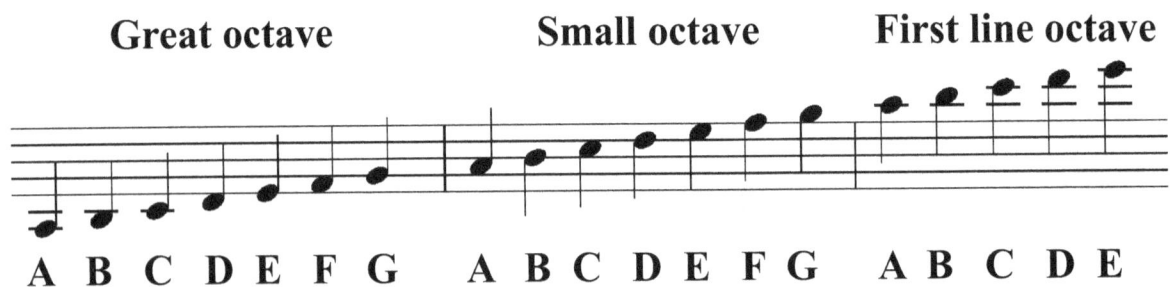

Did you think you learned everything you needed about the PITCHES? That is not the case.

You've probably seen some confusing marks in sheet music. They're called accidentals. Thanks to them, the harmony in the music of the last four hundred years has become more and more varied and rich.

Accidentals

♯ **Sharp** raises the pitch of a note by one semitone.

♭ **Flat** lowers the pitch of a note by one semitone.

𝄪 **Double sharp** raises the pitch of a note by one tone (or a step).

♭♭ **Double flat** lowers the pitch of a note by one tone (or a step).

♮ **Natural** cancels the effect of sharps and flats, including the double ones.

The position of a note on the stave indicates its **PITCH**, but there is also such a thing as **DURATION**. These are the main types of durations:

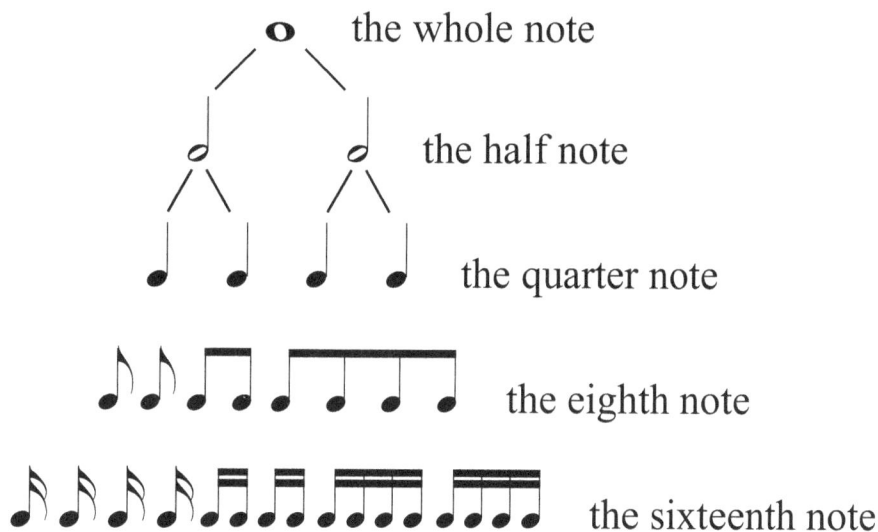

the whole note

the half note

the quarter note

the eighth note

the sixteenth note

Also, in music, there is such a thing as **REST**. The rests are equal to durations, but they are marked differently. During a **REST**, the count does not stop, but there is no sound being extracted. Here are the basic ones:

the whole rest = 𝅝

the half rest = 𝅗𝅥

♩ the quarter rest = ♩

♪ the eighth rest = ♪

♪ the sixteenth rest = ♬

A measure is a minimal segment of a piece of music within **the bar lines.**

Time signature indicates the number of durations in a measure. It is denoted by a fraction, where the upper digit represents the number and the lower digit represents the duration. There can be a lot of of different time signatures. The basic ones are 2/4, 3/4, 4/4, 6/8. The others are used much less frequently.

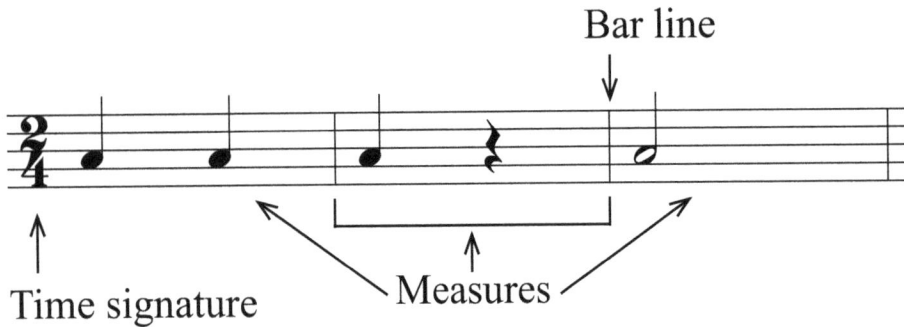

A dot is placed after the note to indicate a change in the duration of a note. The dot adds half of the value of the note to itself. For example, a dotted half note gets 3 beats—the value of a half note is 2, half of 2 is 1 so 2 + 1 = 3.

Clap the rhythm while counting

16

Dotted rhythms mix longer dotted notes with shorter undotted notes.

1 and   2 and   3 and   4 and

= = 1 beat

Clap the rhythm while counting

$\frac{4}{4}$

1 & 2 & 3 & 4 &   1 & 2 & 3& 4 &   1 & 2 & 3& 4& 1& 2& 3& 4&

Key Signatures

Usually certain sharps or flats are used throughout the piece. Writing in those sharps or flats every time they appear takes time and adds clutter. Instead, composers put them in a key signature found just after the clef at the beginning of each stave. Key signatures tell us what notes are always sharp or flat in a given piece of music. Always read the sharps or flats in a key signature. Key signatures always have the sharps and flats listed in the same order. They always follow the same pattern.

The sharps ♯

F♯   G♯   C♯

The flats ♭

E♭   A♭   B♭   E♭

Natural ♮

F♯ F♯ F♯ F

17

♮ This sign overrides all previous signs (flats or sharps) in a measure.

Repetition

Repeat signs

These signs enclose a passage that is to be played twice.

First and second endings

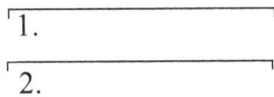

A repeated passage is to be played with a different endings on the second time.

Section 3.
Breathing. Breathing Exercises

In my opinion, the very first thing you need to know to start learning the French horn is how to breath properly. Without this skill, further training will be overly prolonged and accompanied by a series of mistakes that may even lead to a performer being unfit for the profession.

The French horn player's performance breathing is quite different from normal breathing. When playing the instrument, you need to inhale a lot and quickly, but the exhalation will most often be quite long and always against the resistance created by the instrument.

I want to introduce the reader to some basic breathing exercises that I use in my teaching practice.

1. Arm swings (video 1)
Recommended for activating the entire respiratory system.
Place your feet at shoulder width, bend forward and then straighten up, taking a deep breath, and spread your arms out to the sides. Then, as you exhale, lower your torso down, with your arms hanging between your legs. Then, inhaling deeply, straighten up and spread your arms out to the sides. Repeat these two actions, gradually accelerating the speed, until you feel **light-headed.**
The exercise should not be performed for more than 1 minute.

1, 2, 3, 4*

2. Exercise for a brass player's proper breathing (video 2)
You need a metronome to perform this exercise correctly.
Sit on the edge of a chair and press your chest against your knees, with your arms under your legs. The tempo is in the range from 60 to 70 beats per minute. Inhale for a beat, then exhale for one beat of the metronome. Repeat this 4 times. Then inhale for 2 beats and exhale for 2 beats of the metronome. Then repeat the exercise for 3 and 4 beats of the metronome respectively. And only after this, straighten up, put your hands on your waist and take a deep breath. If when inhaling, your shoulders do not rise, and the hands on the waist spread, it means that the exercise is performed correctly. To consolidate the skill, you

*See page 62 for all videos and audio files.

need two to four weeks of daily repetition of this exercise.

The duration of the exercise is two to four minutes.

3. Breathing with the mouth wide open and the palm of the hand pressed over its middle (video 3)

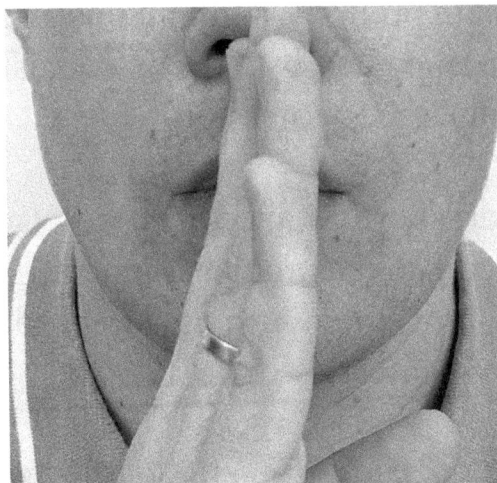

The tempo of this exercise is 60 beats per minute. Inhale and exhale four times with each set divided into quarter notes, eighth notes, triplets, and sixteenth notes. Note: it is necessary to ensure proper performance breathing. Muscles should work as in the previous exercise. Shoulders should not rise, and the abdomen and sides should be inflated.

The duration of the exercise is up to two minutes.

4. Archery-like exercise (video 4)

Inhale slowly with an imaginary draw of the bowstring followed by the release of an imaginary arrow, exhaling quickly. Up to 8 repetitions.

This set of exercises is designed for all possible breathing tasks, such as slow inhalation — slow exhalation; slow inhalation — fast exhalation; fast inhalation — slow exhalation; fast inhalation — fast exhalation.

In professional wind instrument teaching methods, performance breathing is divided into phases and types. For example, chest breathing, abdominal breathing, diaphragmatic breathing and other types of breathing. What you should know is that breathing should be deep and without unnecessary tension.

Section 4.
Structure and Types of Mouthpieces

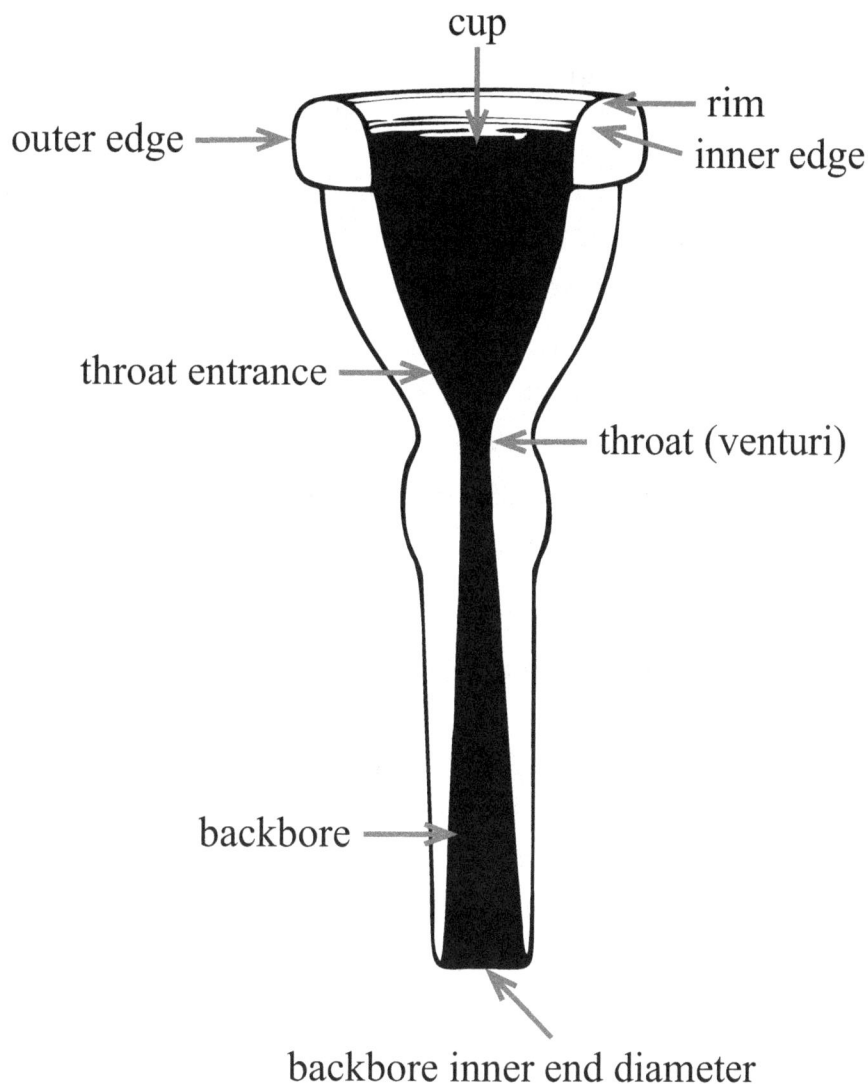

cup

rim

inner edge

outer edge

throat entrance

throat (venturi)

backbore

backbore inner end diameter

The mouthpiece is the part of the instrument that comes in direct contact with the performer's lips, so it's important to know a few rules.

- The mouthpiece should always be clean. Washing it with soap in warm water before practicing is recommended.
- Don't give anyone your mouthpiece. It's not hygienic.
- The mouthpiece should be plated with silver, gold, or at least nickel. If it is made without plating (so it's just brass), it can pose health risks due to the presence of copper, which can form toxic oxides.
- Carry and store the mouthpiece in a tight case or cloth (a handkerchief, for example).
- The mouthpiece is made of metal, but that doesn't mean it will last for-

ever. The edges of the mouthpiece's shank can bend if dropped on a hard surface, and the rim may develop scratches along its surface. It is advisable to have the mouthpiece replaced or restored by a skilled craftsman every few years.

- At least once a month, you should clean the inside of the shank of the mouthpiece with a special cleaning brush.

Mouthpieces come in different shapes and designs: with deep or shallow cups, sharp or rounded rims, and thick or thin shanks. The price also varies.

At the initial stage of learning, it is sufficient to use the mouthpiece that comes with the instrument.

The fact is that in the first years of training the performer does not feel their performing apparatus so well and will not detect much difference. At the next stages of training it is worth choosing a more professional mouthpiece, any from world manufacturers, of which there are many.

The Position of the Mouthpiece on the Lips

The most correct position of the mouthpiece on the lips is considered to be in the middle of the mouth, with the larger part on the upper lip. This can be expressed more precisely by the proportion of 3/5 on the upper lip and 2/5 on the lower lip. This is due to the fact that the upper jaw is more stable compared to the lower jaw. This distribution provides more stability for the mouthpiece on the lips and creates the optimal direction for the air jet exhaled into the instrument. However, all people are different, and other placements could be proper in cases of dental bite peculiarities or other individual differences.

Mouthpiece Exercises

(you will need any keyboard instrument, be it a synthesizer, piano, or a smartphone app)

Level 1. Learning how to extract any sound.

First, you need to figure out how to extract sound. To do this, you will need an ordinary drinking straw and a mirror. Blow into the straw, standing in front of the mirror.

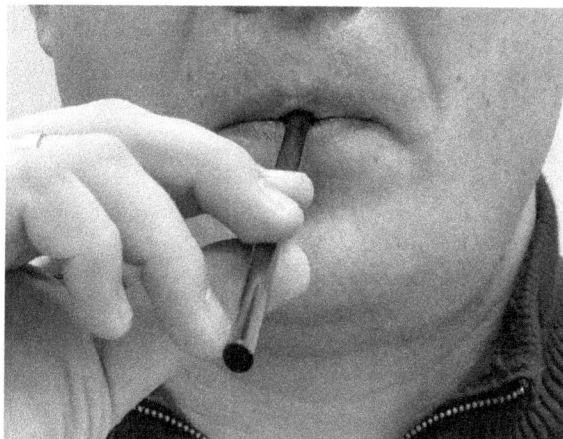

Then remove the straw, but do not stop blowing. This is the position of the lips that you will need to use for further exercises.

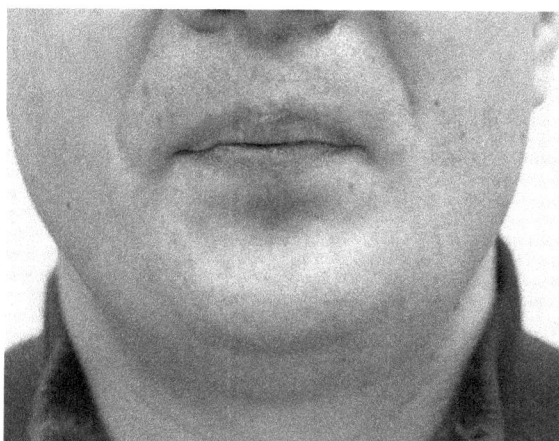

Next, learn how to hold the mouthpiece properly:

1. Take the shank of the mouthpiece with your left hand and put it to your lips (Remember, if your fingers slide down the shank, that means there is too much pressure on your lips).

2.

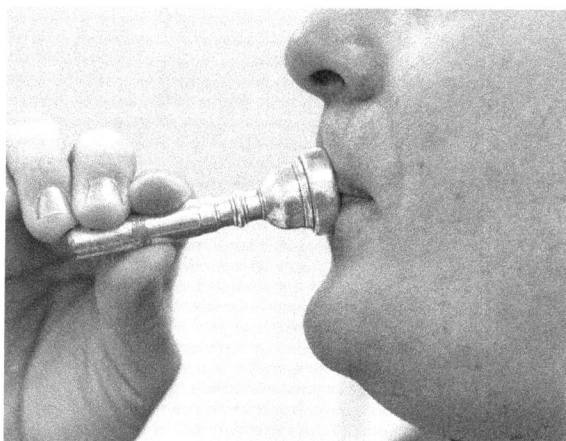

3. Form the lip position you learned earlier.

4. Exhale with a noticeable resistance.

If this is done properly, you will produce a funny sound similar to buzzing (audio 1).

Press any note on your keyboard instrument and try to repeat it with the mouthpiece (audio 2).

1, 2, 3, 4

This exercise is designed to get an initial workout for the lip muscles.

It is important to recognize that any muscle needs to be trained and the lip muscles are no exception. You need a strong lip apparatus to play any wind instrument.

Level 2. Learning how to play three notes in a row (audio 3).

Level 3. Learning how to play five notes in a row (audio 4).

Section 5.
Détaché. Whole, Half and Quarter Notes.
The 3/4 Time Signature

Now it's time to take up the instrument! First, you'll learn what **articulation** is. It's a way of extracting sound. There are a lot of ways of extracting sound. Let's start with the most basic one.

Détaché (a French word meaning *detach*) is performed with a firm **attack** (the beginning of the sound); the sound is sustained to the end without weakening; it is **performed on the syllable TO**. *Détaché* has no special notation in musical notation. Try to extract the note G. For simplicity, I will use letters F and B to denote the fingering.

The sign ✓ indicates where to take a breath

1.

The numbers above the note indicate the number of quarter notes in a measure. Some teachers recommend stomping your foot every quarter note. I teach my students to count to themselves. I recommend that you do the same.

When playing a wind instrument, you need somewhere to breathe. That's why the sign ✓ is often put into the notation. At the initial stage of training, this is necessary. In time, the performer can choose where to take the breath themselves.

Now try the same articulation style, but in **half notes**:

2.

Try *détaché* in quarter notes:

3.

Now it's time to learn how to count whole notes and whole rests:

4.

That's great! Now play the same thing, but use the note C.

5.

Now try changing notes, but after the whole rest:

6.

26

All right! In the next phase, there will be no whole rests. Going forward, there will be no numbers indicating counts for the sake of learning. **A musician should be able to count to themselves.**

7.

Let's combine different note durations using only the note G:

8.

And in a different way:

9.

This concludes the first part of the course. Next, you will see a number of études that will help you to consolidate and develop the skills you have learned.

Étude No. 1 Just two notes. I will indicate the fingering less and less often for the sake of learning.

Étude No. 2

Étude No. 3

Étude No. 4

F 0
B 0

This étude is more advanced and includes the note C5. If you are not yet comfortable playing it, feel free to set it aside for now and return to it when you're ready to tackle the challenge.

The next two études will be in the 3/4 time signature. This time signature is characterized by three beats per measure. I wrote down the count in the first few measures. After this, count along yourself.

Étude No. 5, moving tempo

F 0
B 0

Étude No. 6, moving tempo

Section 6.
Tonality. C major

A tonality refers to a harmonic framework centered around a specific tonic note. Each tonality has its own name, formed from two components: the first is the tonic, and the second is the quality of the scale (major or minor). For example, if the tonic is the note C and the scale is major, the tonality is called C major. Conversely, if the tonic is the note E and the scale is minor, the tonality would be E minor. When you play the notes of a tonality in order, starting from the tonic and moving up to the tonic an octave higher, you create a **scale**.

Practicing scales is the best exercise for mastering an instrument.

C major scale in half notes:

C major scale in half notes, repeating each note:

C major scale in quarter notes:

For ease of understanding, I indicated the fingering as follows: **F at the top, B at the bottom.**

C major scale in quarter notes, repeating each note:

C major scale in quarter notes, playing four notes at a time:

All right! Now that you have mastered these scales, complete some exercises and play easy pieces. **The number of fingering cues will gradually decrease as you progress.**

Exercise 1

Exercise 2

Exercise 3

Exercise 4

Exercise 5

As under the Hill, under the Mountain

Russian folk song

Don't Fly, the Nightingale

Russian folk song

In this piece of music, you encountered the reprise sign ⫾.

It's a repetition sign. In this particular case, it means that the piece must be played twice.

A Fox

Russian folk song

A Little Polka

And now the fun part! **Going forward, I will only give you fingering cues if there are notes you are unfamiliar with.** You will develop the skill of playing without fingering cues.

To reinforce what you've learned, play a few pieces without fingering cues:

Alegretto

W. A. Mozart

Étude No. 7

Étude No. 8

Étude No. 9

Pop! Goes the Weasel

Traditional

Section 7.
B♭ major. *Legato.* D major

It's time to learn other tonalities and articulations. Learn the new scale first:

B♭ major scale in half notes:

B♭ major scale in half notes, repeating each note:

B♭ major scale in quarter notes:

B♭ major scale in quarter notes, repeating each note:

B♭ major scale in quarter notes, playing four notes at a time:

Étude No. 10

Great! Now try without hints.

Étude No. 11

Song

M. Milman

Now learn a new articulation type. As you recall, articulation is a way of extracting sound.

Legato (an Italian word meaning *connected*) is a technique of playing a musical instrument or singing in which there is a smooth transition from one sound to another, without any pauses between the sounds.

Indicated by the mark

The transition from sound to sound is made without a tongue attack, except for the first note.

To (or too)

41

Legato exercises
To be played in C major.

All right! Going forward, the breathing sign ✓ will not be used.
You've probably figured out the logic by now.

Too Too Too Too
Too Too Too Too
Too Too Too Too

Too Too Too Too Too Too Too
Too Too Too Too Too Too Too
Too Too Too Too Too Too
Too Too Too Too Too Too Too

Étude No. 12

Jingle Bells

Traditional

1.

2.

D major scale

D major scale in half notes:

D major scale in half notes, repeating each note:

D major scale in quarter notes

D major scale in quarter notes, repeating each note:

D major scale in quarter notes, playing four notes at a time:

46

Section 8.
Staccato. Eighth Notes. F major

Staccato (an Italian word meaning *abrupt*) is an articulation technique that involves executing sounds in an abrupt manner, creating separation between them. **Each note is shortened by about half of its original duration.**

It is indicated by the word *staccato* or by dots above or below the note heads.

It's simple—eighth notes are half as long as quarter notes.

Étude No. 13

Étude No. 14

F major Scale

It's time to extend your musical range upward.

It may not work the first time, but that's okay. Your lip muscles will get stronger every day you practice.

F major scale in half notes:

F major scale in half notes, repeating each note:

F major scale in quarter notes:

F major scale in quarter notes, repeating each note:

F major scale in quarter notes, playing four notes at a time:

Étude No. 15

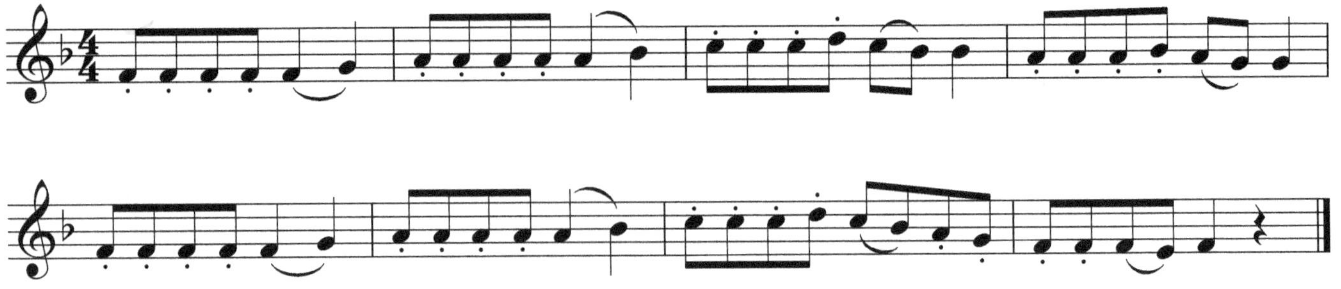

Étude No. 16

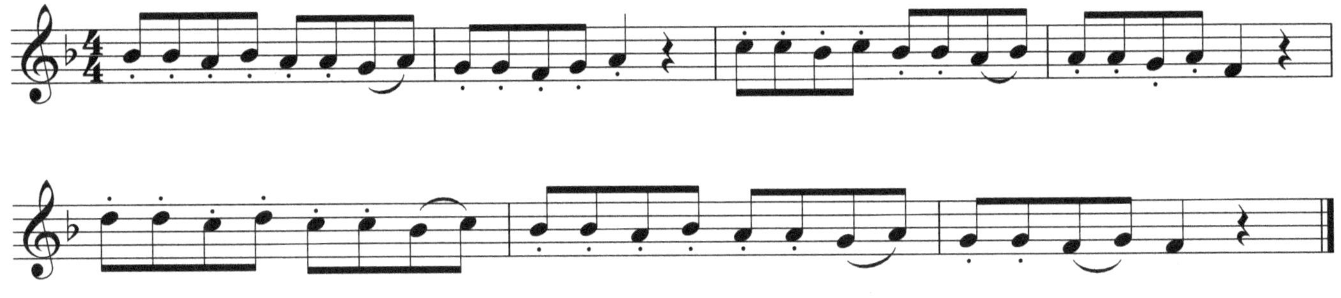

Shepherd Boy

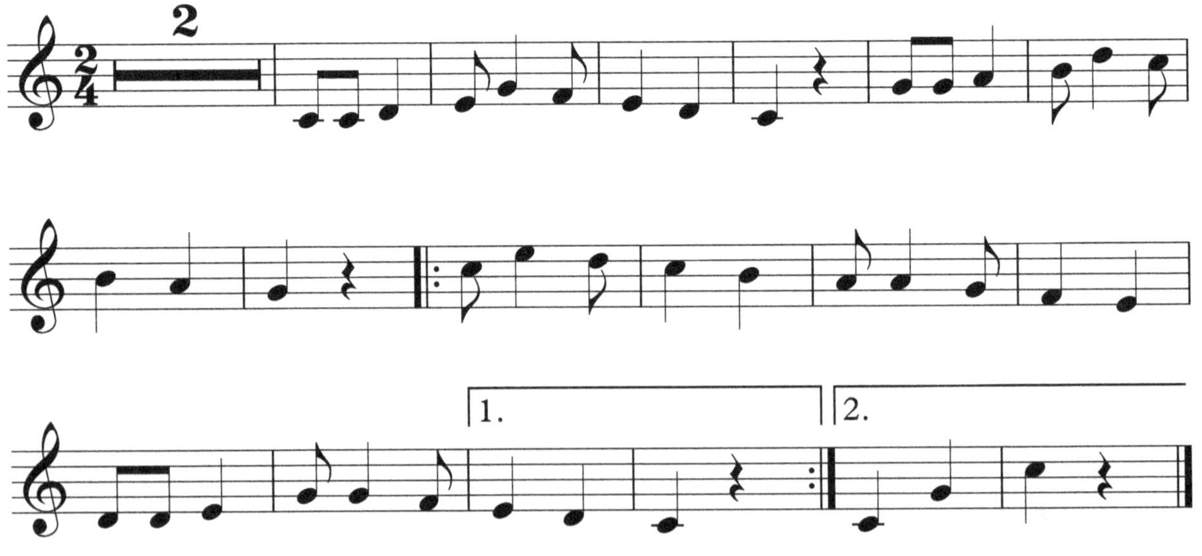

Old MacDonald Had a Farm

Thomas d'Urfey

The Chicken Dance

W. Thomas

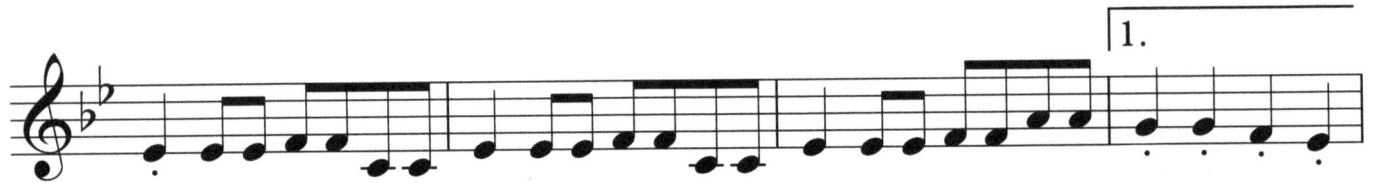

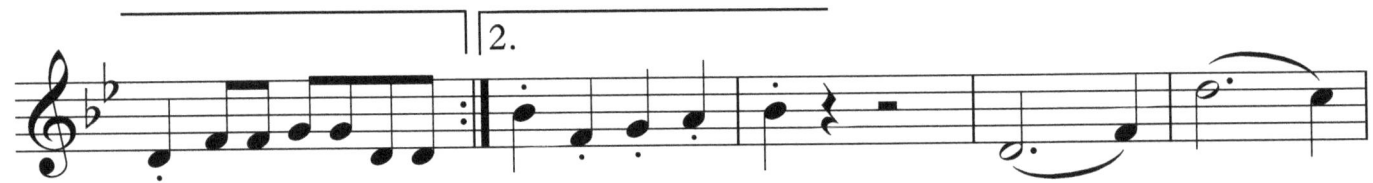

The notes G, A, and B of the small octave (C3)

Now learn about the low notes that appear in some pieces. **To play notes lower than C, you need to push your lips forward slightly.**

These are a couple of exercises to reinforce this material:

Songs

Great job! We've covered the basic articulations and note durations that you may encounter in the initial stages of your learning. Now you're ready to play some ballads, some of which will be accompanied by a backing track.

Scarborough Fair

Traditional

Red River Valley

Traditional

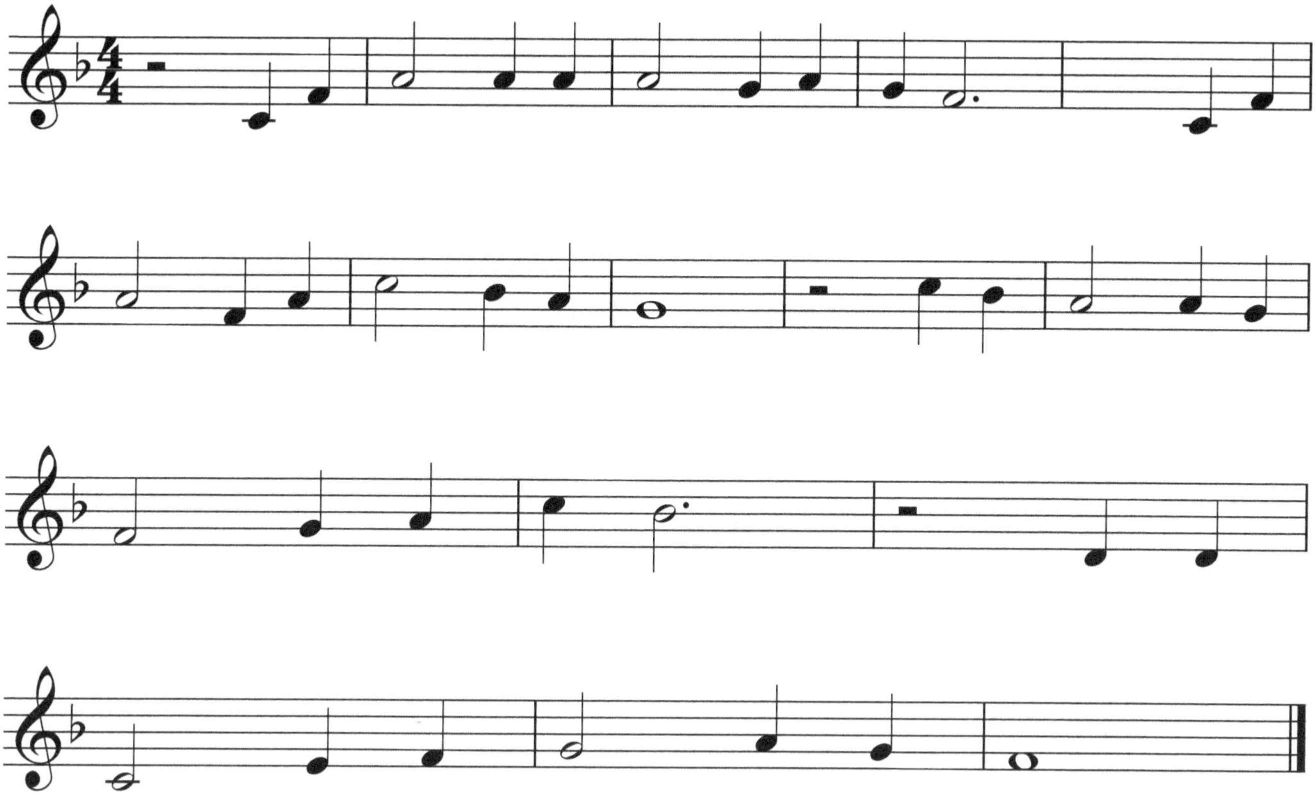

The Flower of Miracles

L. van Beethoven

Songs with Accompaniment

Down in the Valley

American Folk Song

Let Him Go

Traditional Irish

Let My People Go

Spiritual

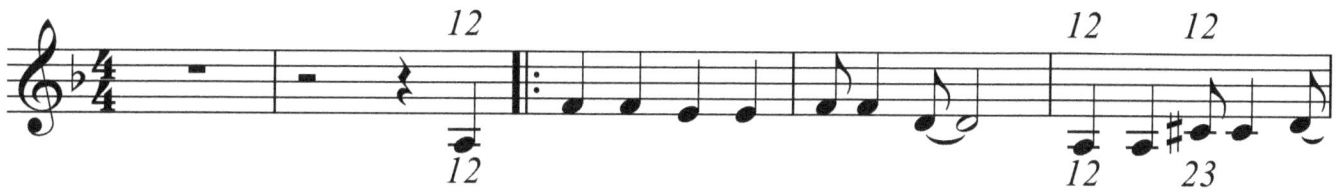

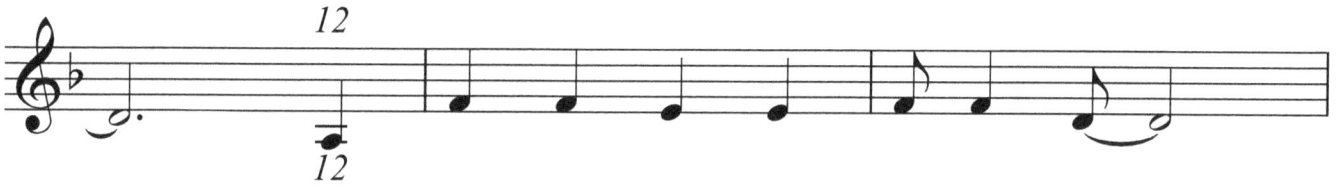

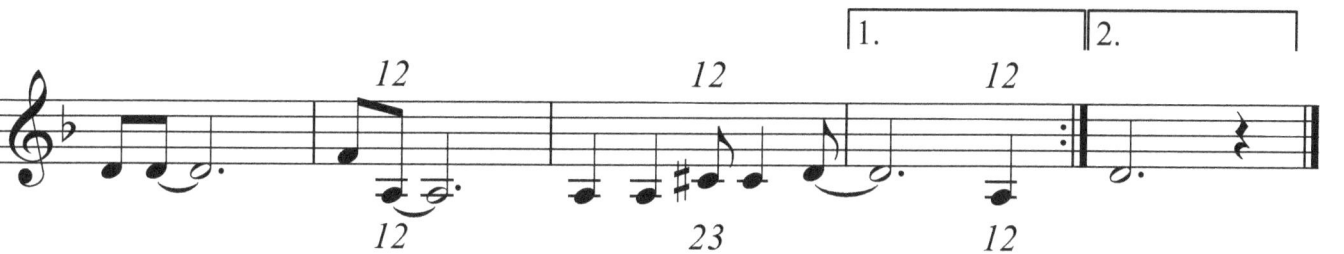

Take Me Out to the Ball Game

w. Jack Norworth
m. Albert Von Tilzer

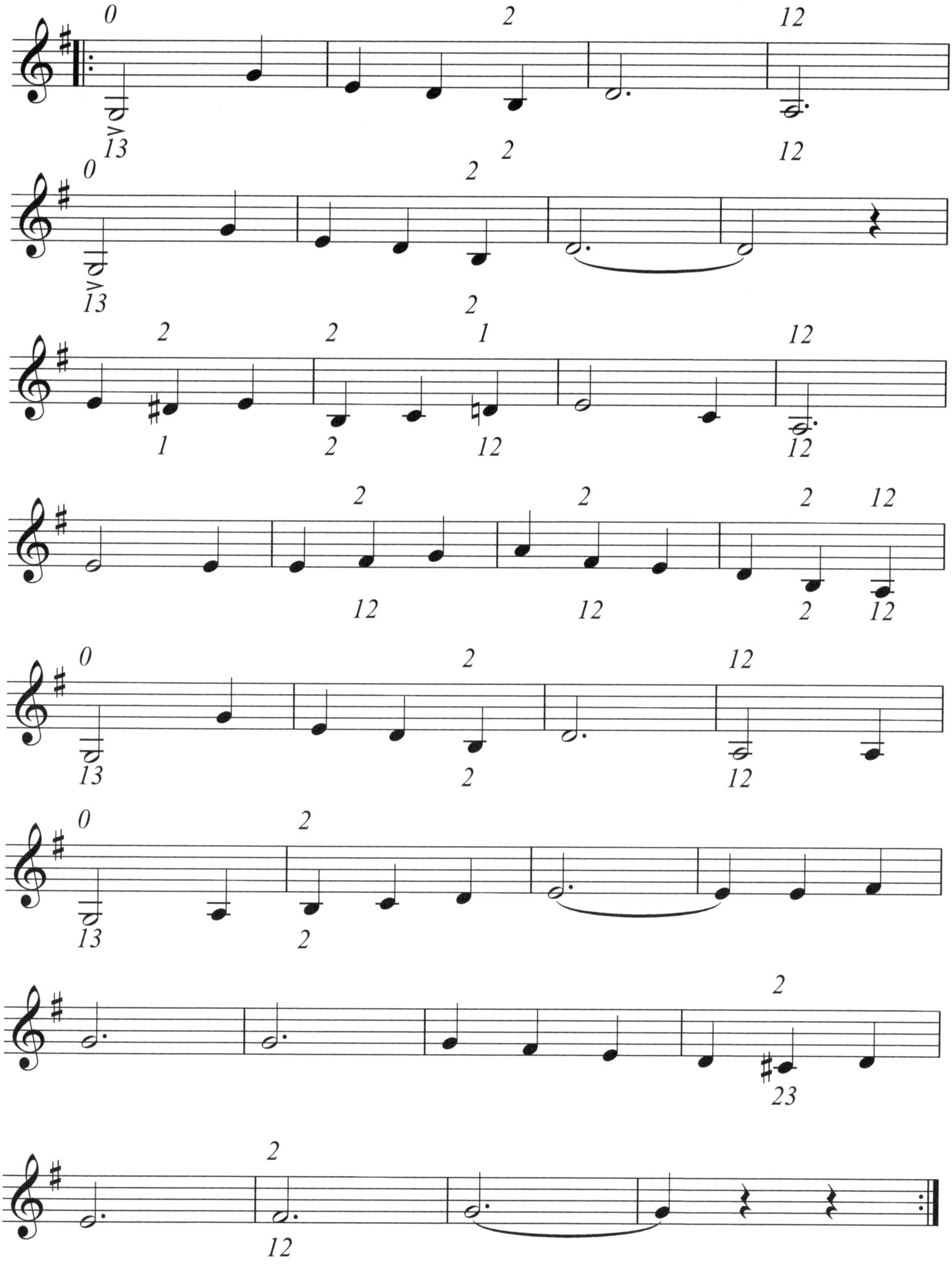

All Audio and Video Files for Downloading

All of the audio and video files are also available on Google Drive:

or use the link:

cutt.ly/ir3QNsKI

1. Important! Be sure to download all files from Google Drive to your computer. We did have a glitch in our system once and our files were temporarily unavailable online. It would be best to download them all at once so you have offline access to them anytime.

2. In songs with accompaniment in audio files marked with "+" sign you will hear an example of how to play the melody (French Horn plays the melody). The audio files marked with "-" have no melody, just the accompaniment track. It is there for you to play along with the track.

For any questions, comments or suggestions, email us at:
albinaopen@gmail.com

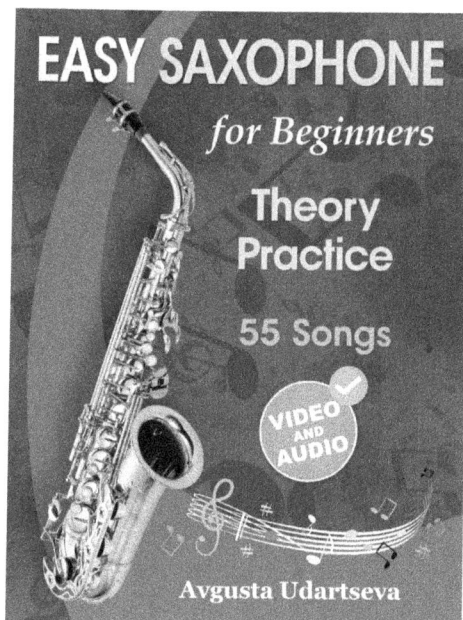

Easy Saxophone for Beginners: Theory, Practice and 55 Songs. For Kids 12+ and Adults. With Online Video and Audio

Complete saxophone instruction book for beginners. For kids 12+ and adults.

This step-by-step guide is for anyone who wants to master the instrument and learn to play their favorite songs effortlessly. The book is also for those who want to learn to swing, play the blues and practice improvisation.

ISBN: 978-1962612098

ASIN: 1962612090

United States   **United Kingdom**   **Canada**

Easy Recorder Lessons for Kids + Video and Audio: Beginner Recorder for Children and Teens with 60 Songs. First Book Step by Step

- Learn the position of the body and hands, how to breathe properly and play easily.
- Letters above each note and simple explanations.
- Convenient large U.S. Letter print size.
- Video accompaniment to all lessons by direct link inside the book.
- 2-in-1 Book: Recorder lessons and video + 60 Songs.

ISBN: 979-8386419004

ASIN: B0BXMX7ZVN

United States   **United Kingdom**   **Canada**

And it's great for adults

www.ingramcontent.com/pod-product-compliance
Lightning Source LLC
Chambersburg PA
CBHW081637040426

42449CB00014B/3350